100 CREATIVE Prayer Ideas for Kids

Other books by Karen Holford

Danger at Deerwood Grove
The Family Book

100 CREATIVE Prayer Ideas for Kids

(and grown-ups too)

Karen Holford

foreword by Aileen Andres Sox

Pacific Press® Publishing Association
Nampa, Idaho
Oshawa, Ontario, Canada
www.pacificpress.com

Designed by Linda Griffith

Additional copies of this book are available by calling toll free 1-800-765-6955
or visiting http://www.adventistbookcenter.com

Unless otherwise marked all Scripture references are from the New
International Version, copyright © 1973, 1978, 1984 by the International
Bible Society. Used by permission of Zondervan Bible Publishers.
Scriptures marked NKJV are from the Holy Bible, New King James Version,
copyright © 1979, 1980, 1982 by Thomas Nelson, Inc. Used by permission.

Library of Congress Cataloging-in-Publication data:

Holford, Karen.
100 creative prayer ideas for kids: (and grown-ups, too) / Karen Holford.
p. cm.
ISBN: 0-8163-1968-5
1. Prayer—Christianity—Study and teaching. 2. Christian education of children.
3. Children—Religious life. I. Title.

BV214 .H65 2003
268'.432—dc21   2002192581

03 04 05 06 07 • 5 4 3 2 1

Thank you

To my parents, Kate and Tony Welch,
who taught me to pray and
encouraged my creativity.

To my children, Bethany, Nathan, and Joel,
with whom praying has been a creative adventure.

To Heather Hanna, Mary Barrett, Heather Haworth,
and all my friends who have encouraged me to
explore creative prayer.

To all those who have come to our creative prayer
workshops and given us feedback and ideas.

To my husband, Bernie, for his help in adapting
the ideas to suit adult small groups and for working with
me in our prayer workshops. Thank you to
him also for buying a special cable so I could
write on the laptop in the car!

And most of all, thank You to God, for giving
us the gift of creativity that adds beauty and
joy to our lives, and also for this wonderful
gift of prayer, so we can develop our relationship with
Him and with each other.

Contents

Foreword

My friend (and now assistant) Anita was starving to death right in front of our eyes. Thin is one thing, but this seemed beyond even supermodel thinness. It was terrifying, and it had gone on way too long.

At first Anita had pain she thought was an ulcer. She had had experience with ulcers. But that wasn't it. It wasn't acid reflux disease or irritable bowel syndrome or cancer. All the doctors she saw prescribed medicine, but none of it worked.

Then almost everything she ate started coming back up the way it had gone down. Now doctors thought the problem was in her head—she was anorexic or bulimic or both.

As her co-workers here at Pacific Press became more and more aware of the problem (it was hard to miss), we began to pray that God would help Anita find a doctor who could diagnose and treat her mysterious ailment.

When Anita's family saw her at Christmastime, they insisted on taking her to Loma Linda University Medical Center. The first doctor she saw was a friend of the family. He said to Anita's husband, Mike, "I don't know what she has, but I wouldn't take her home until I knew." Another doctor told Anita, "Well, I'm sure it isn't cancer. If it had been, you would be dead already."

For three weeks Anita stayed at her sister's home while she was tested and retested at Loma Linda.

Meanwhile, I had gone to a children's ministries convention. One of the seminars I took was on teaching children to pray. Since this was an active learning seminar, we learned about prayer by praying. And one of the prayers we prayed was a "popcorn prayer."

Popcorn prayers are good for a large group of people because everyone can participate—even very shy people—without feeling singled out in any way. Everyone is invited to say a one-word prayer—often the name of a person. At first, just one person speaks, then another, then a couple at a time. Then everyone seems to speak at once and finally the words die down to just a couple. Then one, then another. It really does sound like popcorn popping.

I had never heard of popcorn prayers before, but I knew whose needs were heavy on my heart, and I said, "Anita."

Many, many prayers had already been offered for Anita, so I don't claim for a moment that God answered because I had prayed a popcorn prayer, nor that He answered because the accumulation of prayers was finally great enough. But it was a spine-tingling, goose-bump moment when I phoned the office following that seminar and was told, "They know what Anita has and they can fix it!" Wow.

What she had was nerve damage to her esophagus. Surgery corrected the trouble, and these days Anita's only weight problem is that nagging five pounds most of us would like to lose. (Some of us would like to lose multiples of five, but that's another story for another day.)

I can recall many, many answers to prayer that God has sent over the course of my life, but only few with the clarity of that day, that place, and that prayer.

Which brings me to the reason that I love this book and hope that you spend many hours trying out these prayers with the children in your life.

Prayer is an intimate conversation with the King of the universe. It is as if we have a direct telephone line right to His throne. What's more, each of us has a dedicated line—no one else is allowed to use it. It is exclusively ours.

But to our kids in this modern, visual, fast-paced world, prayer often seems more like sending a wish list to the ceiling of whatever room we happen to be in. And so they pray the same droning litany of requests that they have prayed every night since they can remember. How will they ever learn how incredibly awesome and totally unique is the privilege of prayer unless we spend the time it takes to give it the importance it deserves? Giving prayer our time shouldn't translate into longer prayers for children in worship, but into more thoughtful prayers.

Karen Holford's book can help you breathe new energy into the prayer life of your family or Sabbath School or church school. And while we always want to encourage spontaneous prayer, I also would like everyone I know to experience the richness that can come from prayer experiences that are planned with care.

Perhaps then, when the answers come, they will come with spine tingles and goose-bumps. And they will be memorable. Because we have taken the time to make the prayers themselves meaningful and memorable.

—Aileen Andres Sox, editor

Our Little Friend® / *Primary Treasure*®

How to use this book

Today we live in a world where many people need to experience more than just words in their worship. Many believers find that they can pray in a much more meaningful way when their prayers have a simple structure or include an activity. We can create, explore, enjoy, and even give our prayers away.

We have different interests and styles. Some prayers in the book will suit families and younger children. Some can be adapted for young people and adults.

This is a resource book of creative prayers. Between its covers you'll find prayers for all kinds of situations, and most of them are quite easy to prepare. As you read through the ideas, be open to the Holy Spirit telling you which prayers to use in your situation. But also be courageous and try some of the more unusual prayers when you can. Adapt the ideas freely to your own land-scape and group. The ideas in this book will plant other ideas in your mind, and soon more will grow.

Often it is our own excitement about prayer that can inspire others to pray. Try these ideas on your own before sharing them. Make them a part of your daily worship, and then others will want to experience the creativity and variety that is energizing your prayer life.

SECTION 1

Prayers to Get You Started

Children and adults get stuck often when someone asks them to pray. They may find it hard to know what to say, or their prayers may have become routine. By using a simple but creative idea, you can find a new way to pray, with some new words and different structures for your prayers.

Variety helps in captivating a child's interest in prayers. Start by choosing objects and ideas that are familiar to the child. Many of these ideas will work with adults as well, especially in a small-group setting. Or use them in your own prayer time to put a fresh sparkle into your prayer life!

I

Bag of Bits Prayers

THINGS YOU NEED:
A simple fabric drawstring bag
Lots of bits (items) to go into the bag, depending on your needs

- Here are some examples of bits to put into the bag that will remind the children to pray for different things:
  Photos: Choose photographs of people to pray for, or things that remind you of different people to pray for.
  Plastic toy food: to thank God for giving us food to eat.
  A sock: to thank God for giving us clothes to wear.
  A toy car: "Please keep Daddy/Mommy/us/others safe as we/they travel today."
  A teddy bear or heart: to thank God for loving us.
  A piece of card: A white card that is clean on one side and smudged on the other side. "Please, God, forgive me for …"
  A toy animal: "Please take care of our pets."
  An empty plastic bottle: "Please, God, let it rain on our crops."
  A Band-Aid: "Please, God, keep us safe from being ill." "Please make my knee feel better soon."
- Explain to the child(ren) what each object represents.
- Put all the objects in the bag and let each participant put their hand in the bag and take one or more objects. Take turns praying, using the objects as reminders.
- Return objects to the bag after the prayer.
- Add new items to the prayer bag regularly, and as you are inspired to pray for new things.

ANOTHER OPTION:
- Create your own prayer bag, reminding you of the things you want to pray for.

"Night and day I constantly remember you in my prayers"
(2 Timothy 1:3).

2

Prayer Picture Cards

THINGS YOU NEED:
Index cards
Photos of people
Pictures from magazines
Glue
Clear adhesive film or a laminating machine

- Make cards with different pictures that can remind you or your child to pray for different things, such as things to thank God for, people to pray for, asking for forgiveness and help, and various prayer requests, etc.
- Laminate the cards or protect them with adhesive film.
- Keep the cards together and let the child choose a few to use each time as guides for their prayer.

ANOTHER OPTION:
- Stack the cards in different categories, such as Praises, Thanks, and Requests. Let each person praying choose one or two from each pack.
- Or, share them evenly among those praying.
- In a group of adults, ask each of them to bring pictures of objects that remind them of prayer needs, or that they find inspiring as they pray. Let each person talk about their pictures, and then pray together using the pictures as a guide.

"I will remember the deeds of the Lord"
(Psalm 77:11).

3

Body Part Praise

Use your own body to remind you of wonderful things you can praise God for.

THINGS YOU NEED:
A body
A praising heart

Feet: Thank You, God, for my feet. I praise You that I can stand and move around and explore the beautiful world You have created. Help me to use my feet to go where You want me to go. Help me to be the feet for those who find it difficult to walk.

Knees: Thank You, God, for my knees. I praise You for the gift of prayer. Thank You that I can pray to You and worship You in prayer.

Hands: Thank You, God, for my hands. I praise You for the way they are made and all the wonderful things they can do. Help me to use my hands to show Your love in the world.

Ears: Thank You, God, for my ears. I praise You for the many sounds that they can hear. Help me to listen to what You are saying to me.

Eyes: Thank You, God, for my eyes. I praise You for the incredible creation of my eyes. I praise You for the beauty of the stars, the delicacy and variety of a million different flowers, and the comfort of seeing the familiar faces of those I love. Open my eyes to see people the way You see them, and to love them as You love them.

Mouth: Thank You, God, for my mouth. I praise You that I can speak and express myself. Help me to use my words to spread Your love and encouragement in a hurting world.

ANOTHER OPTION:
- Think about other parts of your body, praising and thanking God for them, and asking Him to help you use the part to share His love with others.

"Now as always Christ will be exalted in my body"
(Philippians 1:20).

4

Teaspoon (TSP) Cards

THINGS YOU NEED:
Plain index cards
Pens

This prayer is called the Teaspoon prayer because it uses the letters TSP for the words Thank You, Sorry, and Please.

- Take three cards and write "Thank You" on one card, "Sorry" on another, and "Please" on the third.
- Put these cards on the table.
- Give each person six plain cards.
- On the back of two of the six cards write a big "T," on two more write a big "S," and on the last two write a big "P."
- On the front of each of the T cards, everyone writes a Thank-You sentence to God.
- On the front of the S cards everyone writes a simple sentence saying sorry to God.
- On the front of the P cards everyone writes a "Please, God" prayer request.
- Then place the cards face down next to the first three cards, so that the cards with T on the back are next to the Thank-You card, and so on.
- Shuffle each pile and give each person two cards from each category.
- Take turns reading the cards you have been given as prayers.

OTHER OPTIONS:
- Do this using one card instead of two.
- Let each person read his or her own cards as a prayer.
- Pray in turn, starting with the Thank-You cards. When they have all been prayed, use the Sorry cards, and then the Please, God cards.
- Or, instead of writing, pass a teaspoon around the circle. The first time the teaspoon is passed from person to person, each person prays a sentence "Thank You" prayer; the next time it passes each person prays a "Sorry" prayer; and the third time, a "Please, God" prayer. Anyone who doesn't want to pray aloud can pass the spoon to the next person.

"I urge, then, first of all, that requests, prayers, intercession and thanksgiving be made for everyone" (I Timothy 2:1).

5

Thank You Book

THINGS YOU NEED:
Sturdy white card
Hole punch
Ring binder
Marker pens
Mirror card
Floral and fur fabrics
Thread
Lavender
Photos of family members
Glue

Here's how to make a Thank You Prayer Book for a small child, full of interactive pages.
- Punch the sturdy white card so that the card pages will fit the rings in the binder.
- Decorate the front of the binder to suit the child.
- On each page write, "Thank You, God, for …" and then finish the sentence to suit the page.
- Make each page lively and interesting. Here are some ideas for the pages:

Thank You, God, for flowers. Cut four-inch (10cm) circles of floral fabric with zigzag scissors. Place the fabric wrong side up and fill the center of the circle with a teaspoon of lavender or other fragrant dried petals. Use thread to tie the lavender tightly into a small bundle in the middle of the fabric. Turn the fabric circle over to give you a flower with a fragrant round center and softly gathered fabric "petals." You can cut the edge of the circle to make it look more like petals if you wish. Stick these to the page so that the child can sniff the fragrant flowers. Or use fabric flowers on which you can sprinkle perfume.

Thank You, God, for my family. Cut a cardboard house shape with enough windows and doors for each member of the family. Cut the windows and doors so that they have flaps that will open. Stick the card house to the page with a photo of each family member behind each flap.

Thank You, God, for animals. Cut a fur fabric animal shape and stick it to the card page. The animal could be cut to look like the child's pet. You could place a flat toy squeaker under the fur before it has been stuck down.

Thank You, God, for making me. Cut a rectangle of mirror card and stick it onto the page so that the child can see his or her own reflection.

OTHER OPTIONS:
- Adapt the idea and the pages to suit your child. Look at other children's interactive books to give you ideas for the pages.
- Involve older children in creating a book like this for their younger sibling.

"Give thanks to the LORD, for he is good"
(Psalm 106:1).

6

Rainbow Thank You Book

THINGS YOU NEED:

Colored card, at least one piece of card for each color of the rainbow
Hole punch
Brightly colored ring binder
Glue
Pens
Lots of pictures

- Create a rainbow of thanks by finding pictures of different-colored things to thank God for. For example, stick a picture of a red apple on the red page and thank God for apples, or a picture of grass on the green page, and water on the blue page. Stick a picture of your house or car on the matching page, or a catalog picture of a favorite item of clothing or a toy.
- Punch the colored card to fit the ring binder.
- Place the pages in the binder so that they are in the order they come in the rainbow.
- At the top of the red piece of card write, "Thank You, God, for red things"; at the top of the orange card write, "Thank You, God, for orange things," and so on through all the colored pages.
- Look for colored items to stick on the matching colored page.
- Add more colored pages when the first ones are filled.
- Use the Rainbow book to help your child think of lots of things to thank God for in their prayers.
- Take a page each and thank God for a few things on each page as you pray.

OTHER OPTIONS:
- Have a scavenger hunt to find objects of different colors to thank God for. This could be done at home, in the school, at church, or outside in nature.
- Place the items onto matching colored paper and then thank God for them.
- Adults could try to bring one item from each color of the rainbow to the group, and then thank God for the different-colored items.

" 'Whenever the rainbow appears in the clouds, I will see it and remember the everlasting covenant' " (Genesis 9:16).

7

Paper Chain Prayer

THINGS YOU NEED:
A packet of pregummed, colored paper-chain links
Or strips of colored paper and double-sided adhesive tape
Pens

- Paper chains are made from strips of colored paper about one inch (2.5cm) wide and six inches (15cm) long. The strips are curled around and their ends stuck together so that they form simple loops. Each paper link is inserted through the previous one before its ends are stuck together. This makes a chain out of paper that can be used as a simple decoration.
- Packets of pregummed, colored paper chains can be bought quite cheaply in some stationery and party stores. Or you can make your own by using colored paper cut six inches (15cm) wide. Then stick a strip of double-sided adhesive tape along one side of the paper, leaving its protective paper in place.
- Cut one-inch (2.5cm) strips across the paper so that each strip is six inches (15cm) long and has a small piece of adhesive at one end.
- Stack the strips in different colors.
- Choose one color for praises, one for thanks, one for requests, and one for saying sorry to God.
- Let the children write sentence prayers on the outside of the chain papers before sticking them together.
- Let each child create their own paper-chain prayer.

ANOTHER OPTION:
- Create one long chain as a family or group.

"'They will come and bind themselves to the Lord'"
(Jeremiah 50:5).

8

Acrostic Name Prayer

T H I N G S   Y O U   N E E D :

Paper

Pens

- In an acrostic prayer the first letters of each sentence make a word or name.
- Take a piece of paper and write the letters of your full name down the side of the paper.
- Use each letter to help you write an acrostic prayer to God.

For example:

J—Jehovah God, my Father, I come to worship You.

O—Over and over I want to praise You for Your love.

E—Even when I make mistakes and hurt You, You still love me.

L—Lord, help me to share Your amazing love with others.

ANOTHER OPTION:

- Choose one of the many names of God given in the Bible and use that as the acrostic name.

"I will give thanks to the LORD because of his righteousness and will sing praise to the name of the LORD Most High" (Psalm 7:17).

9

Tree Prayer

THINGS YOU NEED:
A real tree outside, or a small tree indoors
Or, pictures of trees

Use the different parts of a tree to help you pray.

- **Roots:** Help me to be rooted in You.
- **Trunk:** Help me to grow strong and tall in Your love, always pointing toward heaven.
- **Branches:** Help me to stay connected with You as I reach out to others.
- **Twigs:** Please help me to be aware of the people on the edges of my life, who need to know Your love and care.
- **Leaves:** Please help me to bring comfort, healing, and protection to those around me who are vulnerable.
- **Blossom:** Help me to blossom in Your love, bringing beauty, fragrance, and the promise of life into a cold and darkened world.
- **Fruit:** May the fruit of Your Spirit be produced in my life, to be shared with others.

ANOTHER OPTION:
- As a group, pray while focusing on one part of the tree at a time, perhaps even touching that part of the tree, and let the functions of the tree parts inspire your prayers.

"'All the trees of the field will clap their hands'"
(Isaiah 55:12).

10

Animal Prayer

THINGS YOU NEED:
Pictures of animals

- Create a prayer using the characteristics of different animals.
- Use pictures of animals to stimulate ideas.
- Perhaps a child might like to act out the different animals used in the prayer. Choose animals that your child likes.
- For example:

"Father God, You are such a wonderful Creator! I would love to sing Your praises like a canary! I want to follow You as a duckling follows the mother duck. I want to search for You as a squirrel searches for nuts. I want to be strong for You, like an elephant.

"But sometimes I make mistakes. Forgive me for the times when I want to play like a kitten instead of helping Mom and Dad. Forgive me when I copy others like a parrot, and I don't think for myself. Please make me clean and white again like a newborn lamb."

"Praise the LORD ... wild animals and all cattle, small creatures and flying birds" (Psalm 148:7, 10).

11

Weather Prayer

THINGS YOU NEED:
Card
Marker pens
Weather symbols for fog, rain, wind, snow, cloud, sun, etc.

- Make cards showing the different weather symbols. You may also be able to print these out using your computer.
- Let each symbol remind you of a different prayer idea.
- For example:

Sun: Father, may Your love shine in my life, warming my heart. May I spread the warmth of Your love to others wherever I go today.

Snow: Thank You, Father, for taking my messy sins, and making them whiter than snow.

Fog: Right now I see You only faintly, as if through a thick fog. Please help the fog to clear, so that I can understand more about You.

Wind: Father God, send Your Spirit to blow through my life, clearing away the dust and bringing fresh air.

Rain: Thank You, God, for Your rain, washing me clean, refreshing me, quenching my thirst. Thank You that You are the Water of Life. Help me to drink deeply.

"Praise the LORD ... lightning and hail, snow and clouds, stormy winds that do his bidding" (Psalm 148:7, 8).

12

Pray Dough

THINGS YOU NEED:

Any kind of dough: pie crust, bread, salt dough for modeling, or play dough
A baking tray for each person, or foil pie dish
An oven if needed

- Give each person a piece of dough and something on which to place their finished objects.
- Talk about God being like the Potter and how we are like the clay.
- Invite each person to spend a quiet time in prayer with God.
- As each person prays, let them mold their dough into different shapes. Let them feel how the dough can be shaped in their hands and invite them to pray that they will be easy-to-handle clay in God's hands.
- Encourage them to think what kind of shape God might like to make in their lives. Maybe their gifts and talents will help to form the shape God wants. Maybe other things in their life will help to shape them and make a pattern of their life.
- As they meditate and pray, encourage them to shape the dough in a simple way to represent what God wants to do in their life.
- Close the time by thanking God for taking the time and interest to work in our lives to make them into something beautiful for Him.
- If you wish, let each person describe the shape or pattern they made and why they made it.
- If you have used edible dough, bake it to eat, if you like.
- Or, if you have used a craft dough, you can bake it and keep the model as a reminder of this prayer time.

See p. 28 for Pray Dough recipe.

Pray Dough!
2 cups plain white flour
1 cup salt
2 Tbsp. oil
2 cups water
2 tsp. cream of tartar—this is important for preserving the dough
Food coloring (optional)

Add everything to a heavy-bottomed pan. Heat gently and keep mixing well until everything turns gooey. As soon as the mixture starts to come away from the sides of the pan, it's ready. It's important to cook this mixture just right or it will be too runny or too stiff. Knead well, and leave to cool. Keep in a plastic bag in an airtight container, and it will last for months.

"O LORD, you are our Father. We are the clay, you are the potter"
(Isaiah 64:8).

13

Landscape Prayer

THINGS YOU NEED:
A picture of a landscape or sunset from a calendar
Pen
Self-adhesive white labels

This is an unusual way to write a prayer inspired by God's creation.

- Use a picture of a landscape of something that inspires you to praise God.
- Write your praises and prayers on different parts of the picture, relating your words and themes to that part, such as sky, sun, waves, mountains, etc.
- If the picture is too dark to write on, then stick white labels on the picture and write on them.

Alternatively:
- Use a photo downloaded from the Internet or from a digital camera or graphics program.
- Print it in draft format to give a paler picture, or fade the colors using a photo-edit program.
- Handwrite your prayers onto the picture, or print them using your computer.

"For you make me glad by your deeds, O LORD; I sing for joy at the works of your hands" (Psalm 92:4).

14

Shaped Prayers

THINGS YOU NEED:
Paper
Pencil and eraser
Pen

Create a written prayer within an appropriate shape.

- Let the Holy Spirit inspire you with a topic for prayer.
- Choose a shape for your prayer that suits the topic, such as a heart, cross, person, house, church, etc.
- Write your prayer in rough on a piece of paper.
- Lightly draw the outline of the shape you have chosen on another piece of paper.
- Write your prayer within the outline of the shape, either writing from side to side across the shape, or writing in a spiral from the outside line of the shape to the inside.
- Save your shaped prayers. Perhaps you could fill a small ring binder or notebook with them.

ANOTHER OPTION:
- If you are skilled at calligraphy, you could create some very special cards and posters using this idea.

" 'Let your heart retain my words' "
(Proverbs 4:4, NKJV).

SECTION 2

Praise
Prayers

Often when we pray we use the same few words to praise God. Here are

some ideas to help us be more creative as we praise God for everything that

He is.

15

Alphabet Prayer of Praise

THINGS YOU NEED:
An alphabet
A creative mind
A group of praising voices

- Often the vocabulary we use in our everyday prayers seems so limited. This prayer is a way to generate lots of different praises to God.
- Start the prayer by saying, "We praise You, God, because You are ..." then go through the alphabet finding words that describe God, using each letter in turn.
- Find one word for each letter, or, for more creativity, find as many words as you can that start with each letter.
- Each person just calls out the words as they think of them, with the leader calling out the next letter when necessary.
- For example:
  "We praise You, God, because You are Almighty, Amazing, Alpha, Awesome, Blessed, Bountiful, Beautiful, Caring, Creative, Comforting, Daring, Delightful, Dynamic ... etc. Thank you for being all of these wonderful things. We love You. Amen."
- If you find four words per letter, you'll easily find more than one hundred words to describe God! You can even find words for Q and Y and Z when you think about it! For X, substitute words beginning with Ex, such as Exalted and Excellent.

OTHER OPTIONS:
- Work in pairs, finding one word for each of the letters, then return to the group to share your words and ideas, one letter at a time around the circle.
- Write one letter of the alphabet on the top of each of twenty-six sheets of paper. Pin the twenty-six pieces of paper around the room. Give each participant a marker pen and let them write different praise adjectives beginning with the different letters on the pieces of paper. Gather all the sheets together and read them out alphabetically, or distribute the sheets among the group, each person reading out the words on their paper.

"Praise the LORD, for the LORD is good; sing praise to his name, for that is pleasant" (Psalm 135:3).

16

Alphabet Book of Praise

THINGS YOU NEED:
A small notebook with alphabetized sections, such as a simple address book
A pen
Creative minds

- Work together as a group, family, or couple, and write down as many words as you can that describe God.
- Write each word under its correct letter heading: Awesome under A, etc.
- Write a sentence that includes the word to describe God to give it more meaning, applying it to your own life and experience. For instance, "Father God, when I think about the size of the universe, I remember that You are Awesome." Or, "When You stopped our car from crashing into the bridge, You were our Protector."
- Keep this as an ongoing project, seeing how many different ways you can praise and describe God.

"We pray this so that the name of our Lord Jesus may be glorified in you ... according to the grace of our God and the Lord Jesus Christ" (2 Thessalonians 1:12).

17

Kite Praise

Fly a praising kite!

THINGS YOU NEED:
A simple plastic kite
Or, instructions and materials for making a simple kite
(See library books and hobby shops for instructions and materials)
Permanent transparency pens or marker pens suitable for plastic surfaces

- Make your kite or prepare your purchased kite.
- Use marker pens to write a prayer of praise on the kite.
- Fly your kite high in the sky as you praise God.
- Have a kite for each participant and praise God as you fly the kites together, singing praise songs.
- If you have a kite with a long plastic tail, write your praises along the tail.

ANOTHER OPTION:
- Design or decorate your kite with a Christian logo or symbol.

"Praise the LORD from the heavens, praise him in the heights above"
(Psalm 148:1).

18

Balloon Praise

THINGS YOU NEED:
Balloons
Permanent marker pens

- Blow up the balloons and tie the ends.
- Use the marker pens to write praises to God on the balloons.
- Let everyone read what they have written.
- Tie the balloons in bunches and use them to decorate your worship area.

"Let everything that has breath praise the LORD"
(Psalm 150:6).

19

Thank You Box Prayer

THINGS YOU NEED:
A small, attractive gift box for each person (this may be a simple
cardboard gift box, or something more elaborate)
Small sheets of paper
Pens

- Give each person a gift box, a pen, and many sheets of paper.
- Ask them to write something they want to thank God for on each piece
  of paper.
- If you want to, let each person share some of the more unusual things
  they want to thank God for.
- Let each person fold their slips of paper and put them into their gift box.
- Have an open prayer of thankfulness, in which anyone can say a word or a
  sentence in gratitude to God.
- Encourage them to reopen their "Thank You" boxes and add more slips of
  paper at any time.

OTHER OPTIONS:
- Use a larger box and put in different items that represent some of the
things you want to thank God for. Do this as an individual, family, or group.

- Fill a box with "Thank You" slips of paper as a group. See how many things
you thank God for!

"Praise the LORD, O my soul, and forget not all his benefits"
(Psalm 103:2).

20

Psalm Shout Praise

This is best experienced with a group of friends.

THINGS YOU NEED:
A psalm of praise, such as Psalm 103 or Psalm 136

- Read the psalm, one phrase at a time.
- After each phrase, pause and think about the meaning of the words.
- After your short meditation, shout aloud, "Hallelujah!" or "Praise You, O Lord!"
- Then read the next phrase. Meditate. And shout aloud your praise phrase again.

ANOTHER OPTION:
- Lively children enjoy this kind of praise, and they can choose the praise phrase they want to use, and maybe even clap and jump at the same time as they shout their praises.

"Shout for joy and gladness"
(Psalm 35:27).

21

Flag Praise

Create flags of praise to wave for God's glory!

THINGS YOU NEED:
Plant stakes
Sticky tape
Paper
Marker pens
Beads that fit onto the plant sticks

- Design flags that praise God.
- Draw them on paper and color with marker pens.
- Stick a bead onto the end of the plant stake to protect people from the sharp point.
- Attach the flags to the plant stakes with sticky tape.
- Wave the flags and sing praises to God!

OTHER OPTIONS:
- Make the flags from plastic bags and draw designs with permanent marker pens, or cut out shapes from other plastic bags and stick onto the flag.
- Make the flags with fabric scraps.
- Make streamers to swirl, using long strips of wide ribbon. Write praises to God on the ribbon with fabric marker pens and set with an iron. Attach ribbons to dowel handles, using a special universal swivel attachment from a fishing tackle store so that the ribbon can move freely and doesn't get tangled. Swirl the streamers to make patterns.

"They took palm branches and went out to meet him, shouting, 'Hosanna!' " (John 12:13).

22

Creation Praise

Through this prayer, experience the Creation process and focus on being recreated by God.

THINGS YOU NEED:
A glass of water
Grass to walk on
Flowers to see
Birds to listen to
Perhaps fish or animals to watch
Somewhere to sit and rest
Or
Beautiful photographs of nature
Or
A creative imagination

DAY 1—LIGHT AND DARK
- Shut your eyes and see how dark it can be. Praise God for the dark hours when it's easier to sleep.
- Open your eyes and see the light. Look at all the colors around you. Look for something of every color of the rainbow. Praise God for the whole spectrum of created light that bathes our world with color.

DAY 2—AIR AND WATER
- Fill your lungs with air, and take some deep breaths. Praise God for clear, fresh air.
- Take a drink of pure, cool water. Praise God for water, refreshing and life-giving.

DAY 3—GRASS, FLOWERS, AND TREES
- If you can, walk with bare feet on soft grass. Feel it, soothing, under your feet. Praise God for covering the world with velvety green grass, to make the earth feel comforting and sweet.
- Look closely at a flower, noticing all the details. Breathe in its fragrance. Praise God for the variety of flowers, their exquisite designs, their delicate aromas, and the sparkle they scatter over the world's greenery.

- Look at a tree, strong and tall, rising to the sky. Feel its rough bark and explore its frondy leaves. Praise God for trees, their different shapes, their amazing uses, and their friendly shade.

DAY 4—SUN, MOON, AND STARS

- Feel the sun on your skin, or imagine its warmth on your face. Praise God for the sun that glows over the earth, giving life and joy.
- Think about the cool curve of the moon. Praise God for the simple, rhythmic beauty of the moon at night.
- Think about the glittering sprinkle of stars above your home at night. Praise God for the immensity of the universe, beyond our comprehension.

DAY 5—BIRDS AND FISH

- Listen for the song of a bird. Praise God for the natural music that fills our air, dissolving the silence of the world.
- Think about the fish and all the wonderful things that live in the sea. Praise God for the life hidden deep in the ocean that human beings may never see, and for His amazing creativity in filling even the darkest corners of the earth with His creatures.

DAY 6—ANIMALS AND PEOPLE

- Think about your favorite animal. Think about its special features, the funny things it does. Praise God for the sense of humor with which He created so many of the animals, like a rabbit, giraffe, a duck-billed platypus or an elephant.
- Think about the people you love. Think about the things they have done for you that have helped you to feel especially loved. Think of how much you appreciate their love and concern. Praise God for friends and family, and the joy of togetherness.

DAY 7—REST AND REFLECTION

- Sit down and rest. Relax and just experience the joyful peace of time with God. Just "be" with Him, sensing His love for you, His own unique creation.
- Praise God for everything that He is, and the wonder of knowing that you are made by His hands.

"All you have made will praise you, O LORD"
(Psalm 145:10).

SECTION 3

Prayers for When We Need Forgiveness

Prayers for forgiveness are often the hardest prayers to pray, but they are very important prayers. Here are some different ways to help us pray when we need to ask for forgiveness.

23

Muddy Stone Prayer

THINGS YOU NEED:
A place where you can look for muddy stones
Rubber gloves to keep hands clean
Or, small plastic bags to use for picking up stones
Bucket of water or nearby stream
Sponge
Large wooden or cardboard cross shape if the ground is not suitable for
drawing on

- Find a place where you can go in search of stones that have dried mud stuck to them.
- Send each person to find his or her own muddy stone. The stone represents our lives, muddied by sin.
- Bring the stones back to the group, and sit in a circle around a small cross that has been drawn in the dirt. Place the bucket of water and sponge close by.
- Spend time silently looking at the muddy stone and thinking about the mistakes you have made. Ask God for His forgiveness through Jesus Christ.
- When you are ready, take your stone to the bucket or stream and wash it completely clean.
- Hold your clean stone as you thank God silently for forgiving you for your sins.
- When you have finished, place your stone on the cross that has been drawn on the ground.
- When all the stones have been placed on the cross, the leader can say a short prayer of thanksgiving for the gift of forgiveness through Jesus Christ.
- Don't forget to wash your hands well afterwards.

"If we confess our sins, he is faithful and just and will forgive us our sins and purify us from all unrighteousness" (I John 1:9).

24

Climbing the Hill Prayer

THINGS YOU NEED:
A hill
Some large stones
Good walking shoes
Backpacks (optional)

This prayer activity is a symbol for the way Jesus' forgiveness releases us from the burden of our sins and sets us free. It is best done as a group, but could also work for individual reflection and prayer.

- Start your walk up the hill by meeting together at the bottom of the hill where there are large stones.
- Let each person choose a large stone to carry up the hill. The stone needs to be weighty, but not too awkward to carry.
- The stones represent the burden of our sins in our lives, and may be carried by hand, or in a backpack.
- Walk together quietly up the hill, meditating on the different impacts that sin has had in your life.
- At the top of the hill gather together and put down your stones.
- Place them in a pile, like an altar.
- Gather around the pile and pray together, thanking God for providing a way for us to be free from our sins through Jesus.
- Celebrate your freedom by enjoying a run down the hill for a short way! Perhaps you could shout "Hallelujah!" or sing a chorus about Jesus taking away our sins.

ANOTHER OPTION:
- Choose stones to represent your burden of sin, but let someone else carry your burden for you, while you carry theirs up the hill. How does it feel to bear someone else's burdens?

"Cast your burden on the LORD, and He shall sustain you"
(Psalm 55:22, NKJV).

25

Sandy Confessions

THINGS YOU NEED:
A sandy shore
Small sticks

This prayer can be prayed as an individual, or as a group. It symbolizes how Jesus washes away our sins, and echoes the story of Jesus writing in the dust when the Pharisees brought Him the woman caught in adultery.

- Gather on a sandy beach, ideally when the tide is coming in.
- Give each person a stick and plenty of space for privacy.
- Let them write some words or symbols that represent their sins in the sand just where the waves are washing in and out.
- As they pray quietly, confessing their sins, let them watch while their words and symbols disappear as the tide moves over them and stirs up the sand.
- Then thank God for washing away our sins.
- Always make sure that people are safe during activities close to water and mud. Choose shallow and calm water, and test the safety of any muddy areas.

ANOTHER OPTION:
- Where you don't have access to tidal beaches, find a shallow stream or river with a sandy or muddy bed. Stand in the stream, or use a long stick and stand on the bank. Use the stick to "write" your sins on the riverbed, and watch them disappear as the water flows over them.

"He stooped down and wrote on the ground"
(John 8:8).

26

Clean Feet Prayer

THINGS YOU NEED:
A dusty or muddy area
A clean stream or lake, or bowls of fresh water
Towels
Scented oil or body moisturizer

This prayer activity reminds us that even when we have been baptized, we still need to come to Jesus for regular cleansing. This needs to be done as a group, or in pairs.

- Let everyone take off their footwear and walk in the mud and dirt for a while, as they reflect on how sin has muddied up their lives.
- Let everyone find a partner, or make up a threesome if there is an odd number of people.
- Wash each other's feet, mirroring Jesus' act of love for His disciples. Use the natural water, or collect water in bowls to make it easier.
- When you have washed your partner's feet, dry them carefully with a towel, and then "anoint" them with fragrant oil or moisturizer.
- Pray for your partner, silently or aloud, thanking God for His forgiveness for your partner, and praying that God will strengthen them to resist temptation.

"He poured water into a basin and began to wash his disciples' feet, drying them with the towel that was wrapped around him" (John 13:5).

27

The Balloon Prayer

Very small children, or those who don't like to be startled, may wish to avoid this activity.

THINGS YOU NEED:
A packet of balloons, enough for one to each person
A balloon inflator
Overhead-transparency pens, one for each person
Pins

- Blow up one balloon for each person, plus a couple of extras for mishaps.
- Give each person a balloon and a pen.
- Let them write their prayers of confession on the balloons.
- Let each person hold his or her own balloon and keep it safe until everyone is ready.
- Have a prayer of confession as a group.
- Then pop the balloons using pins, or by jumping on them.
- Pray again, thanking God for His forgiveness.
- Collect all the balloon scraps and throw them away where small animals and children won't swallow them.

"I write to you, dear children, because your sins have been forgiven on account of his name" (1 John 2:12).

28

Patchwork Cross Prayer

This is a good activity for a group to do together around a table, with a wooden cross in the center, and the materials scattered around so that everyone can reach the paper and glue.

THINGS YOU NEED:
A cross made from wood, with flat surfaces
Coordinated scraps of colored paper, or wrapping paper printed with a small design
Decoupage glue (or use slightly diluted PVA glue)
Brushes for the glue
Pencils

- Let everyone choose some scraps of paper.
- Each person writes on the back of the different scraps of paper the things for which they need forgiveness.
- The edges of the scraps of paper can be torn for best effect.
- When people are ready they can come to the cross and paste their scrap paper onto the wood.
- The scraps are pasted down with their writing on the side that is stuck to the cross, so that no one sees what they have written.
- Pieces can overlap so that all the wood is covered.
- If some parts are not covered when everyone has stuck their paper down, work together as a group tearing paper scraps and sticking them onto the front and sides of the cross until it is completely covered.
- Coat the cross with another layer of the glue to protect it and give it a shiny finish.
- Stand the cross up carefully and leave it to dry.
- Explain that our sins have moved from us to the cross, where Christ has dealt with them.
- Have a group prayer for forgiveness, thanking God for Jesus' victory over sins on the cross.

OTHER OPTIONS:
- Use a heart-shaped piece of wood.

- Write on the back of smooth stones or pressed leaves and stick them onto the cross.
- Write on the back of mosaic tiles and use tile adhesive and grouting to complete the cross.

"In him we have redemption through his blood, the forgiveness of sins, in accordance with the riches of God's grace that he lavished on us with all wisdom and understanding" (Ephesians 1:7, 8).

Washed Away Prayer

THINGS YOU NEED:
Squares of white cotton fabric
Water-soluble pens from a needlecraft store
(Check the pen instructions for the best way to dissolve the ink.)
Bowl of water

- Let each person write a prayer for forgiveness onto a scrap of white fabric using the water-soluble pens.
- Then place all the fabric squares in the bowl of water.
- Stand around the bowl of water and pray for forgiveness.
- Take out the fabric squares, which should be all white again by now. If not, stir the squares in the water until all of them are clean.
- Praise God for taking our stained and messy lives and washing them whiter than snow!

"Wash me, and I will be whiter than snow"
(Psalm 51:7).

30

Bubble Prayer

THINGS YOU NEED:
A pot of children's bubble liquid

- Think for a while about the times when you have made mistakes and sinned.
- When you are ready, take the bubble pot. Pray quietly, telling God that you are giving Him your sinful parts, and, after you have prayed, blow a stream of bubbles.
- The bubbles represent your letting go of your sins.
- Just as the bubbles pop and disappear, God is taking care of your sins and making them disappear without a trace.

"Therefore, there is now no condemnation for those who are in Christ Jesus" (Romans 8:1).

31

Stones in the Sea Prayer

THINGS YOU NEED:
A beach with pretty stones
A lake, river, or ocean

- Tell everyone to find an attractive stone, one they really like.
- Let them hold it for a while. Tell them that this represents a favorite sin.
- Spend some time individually, quietly talking to God about the challenge of letting go of your favorite sin.
- Then come together and throw your stones into the deep water where they can never be found.
- Remember that God takes our sins and buries them in the deepest ocean, so that no one can ever find them again.
- Spend time praising God for taking away our sins.

"As far as the east is from the west, so far has he removed our transgressions from us" (Psalm 103:12).

SECTION 4

New Ways With
the Lord's Prayer

A familiar prayer can lose its meaning quite easily, but by finding a new way

to pray the Lord's Prayer, we can discover fresh meanings.

The Lord's Prayer With Actions

THINGS YOU NEED:
An active body
A Bible opened to Matthew 6:9-13

Use the actions described below as you say the words of the Lord's Prayer.

- "Our" (point both hands to the chest)
- "Father" (hug own body)
- "Who art in heaven" (raise both hands upwards)
- "Hallowed be Thy name" (place hands together in prayer)
- "Thy kingdom come" ("pull" heaven down out of the sky to your chest with both hands)
- "Thy will be done" (with elbows into your side touch your shoulders with both hands at the same time, left hand to left shoulder, right to right, then lower both hands, as if offering them, until they are at a ninety-degree angle from the body)
- "On earth" (spread hands down toward ground and around, indicating the earth)
- "As it is in heaven" (spread hands up and around to indicate heaven).
- "Give us this day" (start with hands out in a receiving position, then draw them inward and close the fists at the same time)
- "Our daily bread" (using left hand as a piece of bread, use right index and middle fingers together to perform the action of spreading butter back and forth across the left hand)
- "And forgive us our sins" (use both hands in a motion of flinging something away)
- "As we" (point to self with both hands)
- "Forgive those" (repeat forgiving action above).
- "Who sin against us" (clench both fists, and bang the right one down on top of the left one, as if hammering it once)
- "And lead us not into temptation" (keeping fists closed, cross wrists as if they are tied together)

- "But deliver us from evil" (pull wrists apart as if being suddenly freed)
- "For Thine is the kingdom" (use both hands, with fingers pointing upwards, to make a crown for your head)
- "The power" (use both hands to show biceps in a power action)
- "And the glory" (lift arms together over head, and bring them down and out to each side to form a glorious circle)
- "Forever and ever" (arms move in two steps out to each side, simultaneously, as if drawing a rounded M-shape)
- "Amen" (hands come together in prayer)

33

The Personalized Lord's Prayer

THINGS YOU NEED:
Paper and pencil (optional)
Bible opened to Matthew 6:9-13

Take each portion of the Lord's Prayer and personalize it to your situation. Perhaps you could expand each phrase to make it apply to your life. For example:

"My Daddy who lives in heaven, here I am, Your child. I just want to come and sit on Your lap awhile and talk to You.

"I want to praise You for everything that You are—Almighty, Creator, Savior, King, and Friend—all the different names You have that are special.

"I long so much for You to come again and take me to be with You.

"But while I'm here on earth, I want to be a channel of Your love to those around me. Wouldn't it be special if they could know Your love as clearly as the angels in heaven know Your love?

"Thank You for all the gifts You shower on me each day. Today I need Your help as I face a particular challenge ...

"Please forgive me for the ways I have hurt You so badly, and those around me by ...

"Help me also to forgive those who have hurt me ...

"Please protect me when I am close to being tempted. Help me to be strong and make the right choices, and keep me safe in Your arms today.

"You are my King; rule over my life.

"You are my Strength, making up for my weakness.

"You are all Glory. It's wonderful to spend this time with You in Your shining and glorious presence.

"May Your will be done in my life, through the grace of Your Son and my Brother, Amen."

Lord's Prayer Book

THINGS YOU NEED:
A scrapbook or pages and a ring binder
Glue
Scissors
Pictures of all kinds
Marker pen
Bible opened to Matthew 6:9-13

To make a scrapbook or ring binder and pages:
- Make an attractive cover.
- On the top of each page write one phrase of the Lord's Prayer, so that as you read through the book, you read through the entire Lord's Prayer.
- Stick pictures on each page to illustrate the different phrases of the Lord's Prayer.

For example:
- "Our Father who art in heaven" (pictures of fathers and children being loving and happy)
- "Hallowed be Thy name" (cut out attractively printed names for God, or make the names from separate letters cut from magazines, or print the names on the computer in beautiful fonts and colors)
- "Thy kingdom come" (pictures of heaven)
- "Thy will be done on earth as it is in heaven" (pictures of angels, or people helping people, etc.)
- "Give us this day our daily bread" (pictures of food, clothes, home, etc.)
- "And forgive us our sins" (pictures of sad faces)
- "As we forgive those who sin against us" (pictures of people hugging each other)
- "And lead us not into temptation" (pictures of the things you find tempting)
- "But deliver us from evil" (people being rescued)
- "For Thine is the kingdom, the power, and the glory" (pictures of heaven, nature, and glorious things)
- "Forever and ever, Amen."

35

The Lord's Prayer on My Fingers

T H I N G S   Y O U   N E E D :
Two hands
Bible opened to Matthew 6:9-13

- Use all your fingers and thumbs to remind you of the different phrases of the Lord's Prayer.
  1. "Our Father who art in heaven" (left thumb up with fingers in grip as sign of power)
  3. "Hallowed be Thy name" (point with left index finger to heaven)
  4. "Thy kingdom come" (left middle and tallest finger—God is King)
  5. "Thy will be done on earth as it is in heaven" (left ring finger—wiggle up and down, to heaven and earth)
  6. "Give us this day our daily bread" (left little finger—spreading bread action)
  7. "And forgive us our sins, as we forgive those who sin against us" (right thumb sticking up with fingers gripped like "OK" sign)
  8. "And lead us not into temptation" (right index finger pointing to heaven)
  9. "But deliver us from evil" (right tallest finger held up straight next to index finger as if supporting it)
  10. "For Thine is the kingdom, the power and the glory" (right ring finger wiggling up and down for each beat in the sentence)
  11. "Forever and ever, Amen" (right little finger turning in circles)

- Say one phrase as you hold up each finger.

The Lord's Prayer by Candlelight

THINGS YOU NEED:
Ten different colored candles
Or, a candlestick with ten candles
Long matches or candle-lighting taper
Bible opened to Matthew 6:9-13

- Light candles as you say the different phrases of the Lord's Prayer.
  1. Our Father who art in heaven
  2. Hallowed be Thy name
  3. Thy kingdom come
  4. Thy will be done on earth as it is in heaven
  5. Give us this day our daily bread
  6. And forgive us our sins, as we forgive those who sin against us
  7. And lead us not into temptation
  8. But deliver us from evil
  9. For Thine is the kingdom, the power, and the glory
  10. Forever and ever, Amen

- Say each phrase as you light each candle.
- Pause for a moment and think about each phrase before lighting the next candle.

ANOTHER OPTION:
- In a group, let different people light the different candles.

Special thanks to the Greek Mission of Seventh-day Adventists, Athens, Greece, for this idea.

SECTION 5

Prayers Around the Home

By using the simple, everyday things around us in the home, we can find inspiration for new prayer experiences right where we are.

37

Walk Through the Home Prayer

THINGS YOU NEED:
A home

- Walk together, or alone, through your home.
- As you walk through the different rooms, pray about different things. If your home doesn't have all these rooms, use the ones you have, or move to different areas of the home where you do different activities.
- Put aside all the jobs that need doing in the home, and let them rest, so that they don't distract you. Or use this prayer at a time when your home is most likely to be tidy.

Start outside the front door.

Front door
Just as we stand at the front door, waiting to go inside, our Father, God, is waiting for us to come and visit with Him as we pray. Think about how it feels to knock on our Father's door and to be welcomed inside as we start to pray with Him.

Entrance hall or entryway
As you enter the house, put aside all the baggage you are carrying. It's here that you take off your shoes, hang up your coat, put down your things, and sigh with relief that you're back home once again. So mentally let go of all the things that could distract you as you pray, and feel at home with God. Greet God with praises and even a song of joy!

Kitchen
Stand in the kitchen and thank God for everything He has given you. Thank Him for your everyday food. Stand at the sink and thank Him for being your Living Water, refreshing you and giving you life.

Dining area
This is where you can eat and feast on God's love. Think about the differ-

ent ways He has filled you with His love today, and thank Him for the feast He has provided for you.

Living room
This is often where you spend time with your friends and family. Pray for them as you sit in the living room.

Stairs
Ask God to keep you safe as you journey upward with Him, one step at a time. Pause on each step and consider how you can help others to grow closer to God too. Perhaps each step can be a different person or situation that needs God's love.

Attic/basement/garage
As you look at your attic, basement, garage, or under the stairs, wherever it is you store all those extra things, ask God to help you sort out the messy areas of your life, helping you to know what to keep and what to release.

Bathroom
This is the place to confess to God the things for which you need forgiveness. Wash your hands and thank God for washing you clean from all the mistakes you have made.

Bedroom
This is the place where you can rest, relax, and be refreshed with God's love so that you can wake each day with confidence and hope. Thank God that one day we'll all be at home with Him. Wrap a blanket or quilt around you and spend a few moments thinking about how much God loves you before closing this prayer.

"Blessed are those who dwell in your house; they are ever praising you"
(Psalm 84:4).

38

Garden Prayer

THINGS YOU NEED:
A garden, park, or countryside to walk through or sit in

- As you look at the different things around you, in your garden, in a park, or out in the countryside, let the different things you see give you ideas for your prayers.

Path

Jesus, I am reminded that You are the Way. Thank You for making the way for me to be Your child. Guide me on the pathway You have for my life.

Tree

The trees grow so tall and straight, up toward heaven. Help me to keep growing with You. Help me to be firmly rooted in Your love so that I can grow Your special fruit to refresh and nourish a hurting world.

Water

Thank You that You are the Water of Life. Help me to keep drinking from Your living streams. Wash me clean and refresh me with Your forgiveness for my ...

Birds

The praise of the birds is so spontaneous and beautiful. Help me to praise You with the same simplicity and spontaneity.

Let each thing you see—a flower, a butterfly, the mountains—stimulate your thoughts with new ideas for prayer.

"You will be like a well-watered garden"
(Isaiah 58:11).

39

Chore Prayer—1

Use everyday chores to remind you to pray for different people.

T H I N G S   Y O U   N E E D :
A home where there are lots of chores!
Small cards that can be written on and laminated
Hole punch and string to attach prayers to tools

- For example, pray for one person each time you're standing at the sink washing dishes.
- Pray for another person each time you dust, or vacuum the carpet, or mow the lawn.
- Use the boring, everyday jobs as reminders to pray for the people you know.

ANOTHER OPTION:
To help you, you could make small laminated cards with the name of the person and their prayer needs on them, and fix them to the wall near the sink, the vacuum cleaner, lawn mower, etc.

"I remember you in my prayers at all times"
(Romans 1:9, 10).

40

Chore Prayer—2

THINGS YOU NEED:
A home where there are lots of chores!

Use everyday chores to remind you to pray for different concerns.

- When you prepare food, pray for those who have a struggle to find food.
- When you take out the trash, pray for environmental concerns.
- When you do laundry, thank God for taking the stains out of your life.
- When you tidy up, ask God to bring order into your life.
- When you do yard work, thank God for the many beautiful things He has created.

"Pray continually"
(1 Thessalonians 5:17).

41

Around the Table Prayer—Aloud

Pray this prayer at a special meal each week, or at a family reunion.

THINGS YOU NEED:
A circle of loving people

- As you sit around a table, or around a room, take turns to share one joy from the past day, week, or month, or year, and one prayer request for the coming day, week, month, or year. Choose the time span to suit your needs and the group.
- When everyone has shared their joy and their request, each person prays out loud.
- First they thank God for the joy experienced by the person on their right, and then they pray for the need expressed by the person on their left.
- Continue around the circle until everyone has been prayed for.

"Pray for us"
(Hebrews 13:18).

42

Around the Table Prayer—Silent

Pray this prayer at a special meal each week, or at a family reunion.

THINGS YOU NEED:
A circle of loving people

- As you sit around a table, or around a room, take turns to share one joy from the past day, week, or month, or year, and one prayer request for the coming day, week, month, or year. Choose the time span to suit your needs and those of the group.
- When everyone has shared their joy and their request, hold hands in a circle and have each person turn to face the back of the person on their right.
- Silently, everyone thanks God for the joy experienced by the person on his or her right.
- After a short time the leader says, "Amen."
- Now let everyone turn to face the back of the person on his or her left. Spend time silently praying for the special need expressed by the person as their prayer request.
- Once again the leader closes by saying, "Amen."
- Finish with a group hug!

"We have not stopped praying for you"
(Colossians 1:9).

43

Stencil on the Wall Prayer

T H I N G S   Y O U   N E E D :
A plain painted wall
Some old wallpaper
An alphabet stencil
Pencil
Long ruler
Level (spirit level)
Stencil paint
Stencil brushes
Old rag

- Stencil a simple prayer above the bed of your child.
- Choose a prayer from a children's book of prayers, or create your own.
- Using the stencil, practice on the back of some old wallpaper to help you get the spacing right.
- After you have practiced using your stencil on scrap paper, transfer your design to the wall. Use a fine pencil to make guide lines to help you with spacing.
- Dip your brush into stencil paint and dab most of the color onto an old rag, then "stab" the color onto the wall. This prevents drips and keeps the colors subtle.
- You can even shade from one color to another as you stencil, to give the letters a really pretty look.
- Add stencils of flowers, hearts, angels, or other designs to complete the look.

ANOTHER OPTION:
- Use an overhead projector to project words onto the wall, making sure they are straight, and trace the design onto the wall before painting it in with a fine paintbrush.

" 'May there be peace within your walls' "
(Psalm 122:7).

44

Pillow Prayer

Write a good-night prayer on a pillow case for a child.

THINGS YOU NEED:
Plain cotton pillow case
Or, fabric to make up your own pillow case
Pen and paper
Fine permanent fabric pens
Or, water-erasable fabric marker, embroidery threads, hoop and needle

- Write out a good-night prayer on a piece of paper. Or print it on your computer to get a special font style.
- Transfer the prayer onto the pillow case. You may be able to slide the printed design inside the pillow and then see through the fabric. Or use embroidery transfer paper, using the instructions on the packet.
- Use the permanent fabric pens to write and decorate the prayer.
- Or embroider the prayer and embellish it with embroidered designs.

ANOTHER OPTION:
- Make a little pocket in a purchased pillow and hide a prayer for your child to find and read each night.

"'Come to me, all you who are weary and burdened,
and I will give you rest'" (Matthew 11:28).

45

Thank You Diary

THINGS YOU NEED:
A diary with space to write for each day
Pen

- At the end of each day, sit down with your Thank You Diary and write down all the things you want to say Thank You to God for.
- Write them in your diary.
- You can do this on your own, or as a family around the supper table or at bedtime.
- This is a positive way to end each day, as it can be encouraging to think of all that God has done for you.
- Even on a very difficult day you will still be able to find something to thank God for when you search for it.

"Give thanks to the LORD, for he is good; his love endures forever"
(Psalm 106:1).

46

Grace Mats

THINGS YOU NEED:
Thin card
Pencils
Crayons
Marker pens
Laminator

Make a set of place mats for your table with different "Grace" prayers written on them.

- Choose some familiar graces or write your own.
- Write out the graces on the thin card and decorate with pictures and border designs.
- Or, create these using your computer.
- Laminate the card at a printer's or office-supply store.
- Use the grace mats as place mats for your meals, taking turns to say the different graces.

"When he was at the table with them, he took bread, gave thanks, broke it and began to give it to them" (Luke 24:30).

47

What's on Your Plate?

This is a prayer to help you take stock of your life right now.

THINGS YOU NEED:
An attractively set table
A plate, a glass, and a dessert bowl for each person
Slips of paper
Pencils

- Sit each person at the table, with their place set with a plate, glass, and dessert bowl.
- Give everyone several slips of paper and a pencil.
- Let them write out their prayers as follows:

Plate—What's on your plate right now? What are your current issues and tasks? Are there some things on your plate that you'd rather leave to one side? What are they? Invite others to pray with you about these things. What are the tasty things on your plate that you enjoy? Thank God for these things.

Glass—Who or what is refreshing you now? Are there friends who encourage you and support you? What is keeping you fresh spiritually? Share these with others and give thanks for the way God keeps us refreshed. If you feel you're in need of more refreshment, share ideas for how others could refresh and encourage you.

Dessert Bowl—What are you looking forward to at this time? Pray that God will be included in these plans and that everything will work out well. Thank God for the gift of hope.

- Place the written prayers on or in the plate, glass, and bowl.
- Take turns going around the table and sharing your prayers and concerns.
- Pray for each other in pairs.

OTHER OPTIONS:
- This is a good prayer activity for an agapé meal or creative Communion service.

- Use it at a dinner party for your small group, or before a special family meal.

"He has taken me to the banquet hall, and his banner over me is love"
(Song of Solomon 2:4).

SECTION 6

Prayers in Action

Some of us learn and experience things much better when we are doing

something practical. You'll also find practical prayers in other sections of the

book.

48

Fruit of the Spirit Prayer

THINGS YOU NEED:

Fruit bowl with all kinds of fruits. Some examples with their symbolic meaning:

Peach—love (warm, sweet, and soft)

Cherries—joy (bright, cheerful, sweet, even around hard stones)

Banana—peace (symbolized peace in Britain during WWII)

Pomegranate—patience (patience needed to eat a pomegranate)

Strawberry—kindness (willing to grow in humble places)

Apple—goodness (an apple a day keeps the doctor away)

Kiwi—faithfulness (need faith to believe such an ugly fruit can taste good!)

Avocado—gentleness (so gentle even a baby can eat it)

Lemon—self-control (need to be self-controlled when using lemon juice or things can taste sour)

Pencil and paper

- Find ways to explore the different fruits of the Spirit.
- Use the ideas and fruits above, or find your own fruits and symbols.
- Pass the fruit around and meditate as you explore the fruit in your hands.
- Ask God to fill you with His Spirit so that you will produce good fruit.
- Consider how God wants you to experience more of these fruits in your life and in your relationships with others.
- Pray about what you have learned from the experience.

OTHER OPTIONS:

- Serve the fruit cut up in different bowls, each labeled with one of the fruits of the Spirit.
- Write on the label some ideas of how each fruit might illustrate the different fruits of the Spirit.
- Let people help themselves to a serving of each of the fruits.
- Discuss each fruit in turn, as a group, and then eat that fruit as you meditate on its meaning for you.

"The fruit of the Spirit is love, joy, peace, patience, kindness, goodness, faithfulness, gentleness and self-control" (Galatians 5:22, 23).

49

Posters for Prayers

THINGS YOU NEED:
Plain Paper
Marker pens

Create posters to advertise prayer.

- Think of the special features of prayer that you wish to highlight and make the most attractive poster you can.
- Work on this as a family or group project, or on your own.
- If you have all made different posters, introduce your poster to the group and look at the many different aspects of prayer that you've advertised.
- Or you may like to take ideas from current advertising campaigns and themes, and apply them to the special experience of prayer, adapting their images and phrases to portray the best that prayer has to offer.

After all, a relationship with God through prayer is much more satisfying and exciting than any other consumer goods could be!

Other options:
- Make cards to advertise prayer. Pin them on bulletin boards or next to pay phones.
- Put your prayer posters up at church.
- Create a drama or mime that focuses on the special gift of prayer and its power in our lives.
- Write a song together about your prayer experiences.

"Make known among the nations what he has done"
(Psalm 105:1).

50

Love in Action

Turn your prayer into actions!

THINGS YOU NEED:

Paper cut into heart shapes
Crayons
Pens

- Talk together about your prayer needs and requests, and the challenges you are facing in the week ahead.
- Listen to each other and see if there is something you could do to make life easier for someone in your family or group.
- Take the heart shapes, decorate them with crayons or pens, and write a little message on each heart saying, "Love Was Here!"
- Find secret ways to encourage, help, and support each other, praying for each other as you do so, and leaving an anonymous little love heart where you have performed an action of love.
- Enjoy being used by God to be the answer to someone else's prayers!

" 'But when you give ... do not let your left hand know what your right hand is doing, so that your giving may be in secret' "
(Matthew 6:3, 4).

51

Through My Father's Eyes

Seeing people as Jesus sees them.

THINGS YOU NEED:
Spirit-filled heart

- Look at the people around you, especially those you may find hard to love.
- Pray, asking God to help you see these people with new eyes.
- Imagine how God views these people, with His amazing love, sensitivity, and comfort.
- Let God's perspective change your own, transforming your attitude to those around you.
- As you see these people with God's eyes, do for them what Jesus would like to have you to do for them, and put your prayers and new perspective into practice. Offer a kind and encouraging word, a thoughtful anonymous gift, or some practical help.
- Continue looking at people through your Father's eyes. Notice the difference it makes to you, and to them.

" 'As the Father has loved me, so have I loved you.
Now remain in my love' " (John 15:9).

52

Blessings Basket

THINGS YOU NEED:
An attractive basket or pot

- Once a week, count the unique blessings that God has showered on you during the week. Be specific and think about the amazing things He has done for you, helping you through challenges, keeping you safe, answering your prayers, healing your illnesses, etc.
- For each specific blessing, thank God, and add a coin to your Blessing Basket or Blessing Pot.
- Use the money collected in your Blessing Basket to bless others in creative ways, from buying an encouraging card to mail, to paying for a single-parent family to have a much-needed vacation.

ANOTHER OPTION:
- Work together as a group to collect coins in your blessing baskets to sponsor a child, or help with a community project.

"'Freely you have received, freely give'"
(Matthew 10:8).

53

Treasure Hunt Prayer

THINGS YOU NEED:
A home
A creative mind

- Go on a treasure hunt in your home to find things that remind you of God's loving relationship with you this week.
- You can do this on your own, or everyone in the home can go on their own treasure hunt.
- After a certain amount of time, come back together.
- Show the things you have found, talk about how they show you something of God's love, and then thank God for His wonderful love.
- Some ideas to get you started:
    Cotton Ball—God is gentle with me.
    Soap—He washes us clean.
    Seed—His love has grown in my heart.

OTHER OPTIONS:
- If you meet with a group of friends, bring your objects with you.
- Do this as you take a walk through the countryside, and find nature items that remind you of God's love.

"'You will seek me and find me when you seek me with all your heart'"
(Jeremiah 29:13).

Thank You Picture

THINGS YOU NEED:
Preprinted attractive notepaper
Computer graphic design program
Attractive frame

- Write out a list of all your blessings on some attractive paper, or create a design on your computer.
- Frame the paper to make an attractive picture.
- When you feel disheartened, look at the list of blessings you have written and thank God for His amazing generosity in your life.
- Create a new picture when your list needs updating.

"Devote yourselves to prayer, being watchful and thankful"
(Colossians 4:2).

Prayers for Family and Friends

Often our family and friends are the subjects of our prayers. Use the following ideas to make those prayers come alive.

55

Birthday Blessings

THINGS YOU NEED:
A child
A birthday

• When your child has a birthday, take them in your arms, lay your hands on their head, and pray a special prayer of blessing for them, such as the blessing in Numbers 6:24-26.

"The LORD bless you and keep you;
the LORD make his face shine upon you and be gracious to you;
the LORD turn his face toward you and give you peace."

• Perhaps you could write a prayer for your child on his or her birthday and collect them each year in a special book.
• When your child leaves home, present the book to them.
• Maybe they would like to have you continue writing these prayers even when they are adults ... or you could start this over again for your grandchildren.

"And he took the children in his arms, put his hands on them and blessed them" (Mark 10:16).

56

"My Picture" Prayer

THINGS YOU NEED:
Plain paper
Pencils
Marker pens (optional)

A prayer to affirm group members.

- Give everyone a sheet of paper and a pencil.
- Ask them to draw a picture of themselves on the piece of paper.
- Ask them to write at the top of the paper the words, "Thank You, God, for ..." and then write their own name.
- Pass all the pictures around the group and have everyone write one thing about the person pictured that they would like to thank God for. If you want to, keep passing the pictures until everyone has ten things written around their picture.
- When you have finished passing the pictures, make sure that everyone has a different picture than their own.
- Then let each person pray aloud, thanking God for the person pictured, and mentioning all the thankful comments on the paper.
- Return the pictures to their owners.

"We always thank God, the Father of our Lord Jesus Christ, when we pray for you" (Colossians 1:3).

57

Special Gifts Prayer

THINGS YOU NEED:
Pencils
Paper

The final pictures created by this activity are used to stimulate prayers to affirm the special gifts of each group member.

- First, everyone draws their own picture on a piece of paper, with their name underneath it. Make the pictures simple, but try to put in one special identifying feature.
- Then, pass each picture around the family or group.
- When you receive a picture, write on it a special gift you think God has given that person.
- When everyone has written a gift on every picture, return the pictures to their owners so that they can read what has been written about them.
- Then collect the pictures together again, shuffle them and pass them out, being sure that no one has their own picture.
- Whoever is holding the picture prays for the person in the picture, thanking God for the wonderful gifts He has given to the person, and praying that God will help them to use their gifts in special ways.

"Every good and perfect gift is from above"
(James 1:17).

58

Future Prayer

Take time to pray for the future of your loved ones.

THINGS YOU NEED:

Plain paper
Envelopes
Pens
A special basket or box

- Write a letter to God, praying about the future.
- Think about the spirituality of those you love:
  - The friends they will make.
  - The choices they will make.
  - The family they will have.
  - Their protection from harm and danger and illness.
  - The hope that one day you will all be reunited in heaven.
- Don't forget to date the letter.
- Open the letters from time to time, and write new ones. Keep them in a special basket or box. Write prayer answers on the back of the letters, or on a separate card that can be kept in the same envelope.

"May God himself, the God of peace, sanctify you through and through. May your whole spirit, soul and body be kept blameless at the coming of our Lord Jesus Christ" (1 Thessalonians 5:23).

59

Annual Letter Prayer

THINGS YOU NEED:
Plain paper
Envelopes
Pens
A special basket or box

- You may like to write a prayer letter to God each year, on New Year's, or on a child's birthday or a wedding anniversary.
- Each year, open the letter from the year before and see how God has answered. Thank Him for what He has done.
- Write a new letter about the year to come, and thank Him for the ways in which He will answer your prayer.

"You crown the year with your bounty"
(Psalm 65:11).

60

Telephone Prayer

THINGS YOU NEED:
Telephone

- When you are a long way from someone you love, it's good when you can pray together over the phone.
- Just call up and talk through their day, asking if they have anything they want to praise or thank God for, and also about any concerns they have for which they'd like you to pray.
- Then pray a short and simple prayer for them.
- Hearing others pray specifically for us can be very encouraging.

"The LORD is near to all who call on him"
(Psalm 145:18).

61

Family Tree Prayer

THINGS YOU NEED:
Scrap paper
Large piece of paper
Pencil
Crayons
Family Tree
Plain index cards
Adhesive putty

- Sketch out your family tree, showing everyone living. It's best to do this on a scrap piece of paper first, to help you get the spacing right.
- Transfer your family tree onto the large piece of paper.
- Give each named person a space the size of a plain index card.
- Decorate the family tree with pictures of the different people, where they live, or something special about each person. Or draw a large tree around everyone.
- Write special prayers for the different people on plain index cards and stick them onto the family tree. Thank God for each individual person, praise Him for the unique gifts they have, and make your prayer requests for them.
- Pray for your family members regularly.
- Add new prayers and praises as God answers the prayers.

OTHER OPTIONS:
- Create a fabric family tree as a large wall hanging or wall quilt.
- Use special techniques or paper from a craft or print store to transfer photos of the different people onto the fabric.
- Use fabric pens or appliqué to decorate the quilt.
- Sew on clear vinyl pockets to hold the index-card prayers.

"Children's children are a crown to the aged, and parents are the pride of their children" (Proverbs 17:6).

SECTION 8

Prayers for Other People

Praying for other people is an important part of prayer. It connects us with

God and with other people in a special way. Here are some creative ways to

pray for others.

62

Pocket Seeds Prayer

THINGS YOU NEED:
Large seeds such as pumpkin seeds
Permanent (waterproof) ink pen

- Choose a large, smooth seed.
- Think about someone you know who doesn't know Jesus, or is just getting to know Him, or someone that you pray will grow in their relationship with God.
- Using a permanent pen with a fine tip, write the name of the person on the seed.
- Carry the seed in your pocket to remind you to pray for the person.
- Don't forget to take the seed out of your clothes before you wash them!

63

Growing Seeds Prayer

T H I N G S   Y O U   N E E D :
Large seeds, such as pumpkin or gourd seeds
Plant pot
Small stones to place in the base of the pot for drainage
Potting compost or soil
A plant label and pen
Decorations for the pot (optional)

- After writing the name on the seed, plant the seed in a pot and water it well so you can watch it grow.
- Make a decorative plant label with the person's name written on it.
- Water the plant and nurture it well.
- As you take care of the plant, continue to pray for the person's spiritual growth.

ANOTHER OPTION:
- Before planting, decorate the plant pot with paints, raffia, and wooden shapes, perhaps in a style to suit the person you're praying for.

"We constantly pray for you"
(2 Thessalonians 1:11).

64

Flower Prayer

Use a flower to help you pray for other people.

THINGS YOU NEED:
A lovely open flower with a stem, at least one leaf, and a bud

- Choose a beautiful flower and hold it in your hands.
- Use the different parts of the flower to remind you to pray for some of the different people in your life.
- For example:

Stem—Look at the stem. Feel it. Is it narrow or broad? Long or short? Shiny or fuzzy? Even though it's slender, it's often very strong. It supports the flower. Pray for those who support you—your family, friends, pastor, church community, teacher, doctor, counselor, care-giver, etc. Is there someone you know who needs supporting? Ask God to show you how you can support them today.

Leaves—Look at the leaves. What shape are they? How do they feel? Is there one leaf or a cluster? Some leaves contain helpful natural medicines, such as herbs. As you look at the leaves, pray for those you know who long for healing. Pray for those who are sick, injured, hurting, or sad. What can you do to encourage and comfort those you know who long to be healed?

Bud—Look at the bud. It's small and tight, but one day it will blossom into something very beautiful. Pray for those who are small and vulnerable. Pray for the children you know. Pray for those who are studying so that one day they will be able to serve God more effectively. Pray for those you know who are easily ignored, pushed aside, or forgotten, and those who are "budding" spiritually. Are there children or students who need your practical help or encouragement? Ask God to show you what you can do for them today.

Flower—Now look at the flower. It's bright and beautiful. Smell the flower. Does it have a scent? Pray for those who brighten your life with their love, their laughter, and their encouragement. Thank God for the friends He sends to bring beauty, joy, and fragrance into your life. Find a way to let them know how much you appreciate them. Be the beautiful flower in someone else's life.

" 'See how the lilies of the field grow' "
(Matthew 6:28).

65

Finger Puppet Prayer

T H I N G S   Y O U   N E E D :

Purchased finger puppets representing different people familiar to your child

- Place the finger puppets onto your child's fingers and let them look at each puppet as they pray for the person it represents, such as Grandma, the baby, Mom and Dad, their teacher, etc.

OTHER OPTIONS:

- Make finger puppets from cards wrapped around the finger, with drawings or photos of the people your child wants to pray for.
- Draw the different people directly onto the fingertips with a safe, washable pen.
- Purchase a pair of knitted gloves and embroider faces onto the finger ends.

"I want men everywhere to lift up holy hands in prayer"
(I Timothy 2:8).

66

Photo Album Prayer

THINGS YOU NEED:
A small empty photo album
Plain cards that will fit into the photo pockets
Colored marker pens
Stickers

- Choose some photos of the different people you and your family or friends are praying for.
- Pop a photo into a photo pocket.
- Write your prayers, thanks, and prayer requests for that person onto a plain card.
- Decorate the cards with stickers and colored pens.
- Slide the prayer cards into the pockets facing the person's photo.
- As you look through the album, pray for the different people, using the cards to remind you of their needs and concerns.
- Add answers to prayer to the cards, using the back of the cards if you run out of space on the front.

"The prayer of a righteous man is powerful and effective"
(James 5:16).

SECTION 8

67

Prayer Map

Create a prayer map together to remind you of those who need your prayers.

THINGS YOU NEED:
A map of your local community
A large sheet of high-quality paper
Pencil and eraser
Marker pens

- Lay the large piece of paper on a flat surface.
- Draw a simple large-scale map of your community on the paper with the pencil.
- Mark on the map the places that are significant to you and your family, such as your home, your friends' homes, school, church, the hospital, workplaces, the mall, the roads you use, etc.
- Draw outlines of these places on the map, with each outline big enough so that a plain index card will fit inside it.
- Now finish the map with the marker pens, drawing in the main roads, landmarks, parks, etc, to make a colorful map of your area.
- For each significant place on the map take an index card and write your prayer concerns on the front of the card.
- Use removable adhesive putty to stick the index cards onto the significant places on the map. Change and update the cards when necessary.
- Use this map to help you pray for your community and the people you know. Pray for safety as you travel along the roads between the places, as well.
- Add other cards from time to time, to pray for special concerns and challenges in your community, such as victims of violence, factory closures, etc.

"Unless the LORD watches over the city, the watchmen stand guard in vain" (Psalm 127:1).

68

Prayer Card Series

THINGS YOU NEED:
Cards or postcards
Envelopes
Pen
Postage stamps (optional)

This is a way to give someone some daily encouragement. It's good for someone who is ill, going through a difficult time, or in need of special prayer. It's also useful when you are away from those you love.

- Write a series of prayer cards for someone, using postcard or other greetings cards.
- Place each in an envelope and date it to be opened on a different day. Or mail them on different days.
- Try to match the prayers for each day to any special needs the recipient may have on that day.

ANOTHER OPTION:
- You may like to add other little gifts to the envelopes, such as bookmarks, gift-vouchers, stickers, coasters, etc.

"I have not stopped giving thanks for you, remembering you in my prayers" (Ephesians 1:16).

69

Neighborhood Walk

T H I N G S   Y O U   N E E D :
A comfortable pair of shoes
A good pair of eyes
A praying heart
Family and friends to walk with you, although anyone can do this on their own also

- Take a walk around your neighborhood.
- As you pass each home, pray silently to yourself, or aloud in conversation, for the people who live in each home.
- Look for clues to help you know what to pray. Are there children in the home? Does the home look neglected? Does a disabled person live in the home? Even if the home looks happy and prosperous, pray that the people will learn to depend on God rather than on their material possessions. Are there barking dogs and tall fences that may indicate that someone could be fearful?
- If you see people in their yard, greet them with a smile, say hello, and perhaps you'll start a conversation and make a new friend.
- If you pass a playground, pray for the children who play there.
- If you pass a doctor's office, pray for the skill of the doctors and for their patients.
- Find something to pray for each business and building that you pass.
- Pray that the people in each home will grow into an understanding of God's love, and ask God to inspire you with ways you can make friends with, and care for, the people who live in your neighborhood.
- Pray for protection from any evil influences in the neighborhood.
- Repeat the walk regularly, continuing to pray for your community.

"Love your neighbor as yourself"
(Matthew 19:19).

70

Prayer Calendar

THINGS YOU NEED:
A calendar with writing space for each day
Colored pens

- As you talk with your friends and family, write down specific ways they may need your prayers on specific days.
- Pray for them on their birthdays.
- Pray for the days they have interviews and tests, doctor's appointments, special performances, challenges, and joys.
- Pray for couples on their anniversaries.
- Pray for the bereaved on the anniversaries of their loved ones' deaths.
- Pray for your friends on a chosen day each week or month, and let them know that you have a special day to pray for them specifically.
- Pray that you will know what to do and say to those you are praying for.
- Use different colored pens for each person in the family, and ask them each week about their prayer needs for the week ahead. Write them on the calendar so that everyone is reminded to pray for them.

"'Day after day they seek me out'"
(Isaiah 58:2).

71

A Prayer Week

THINGS YOU NEED:
Paper
A pen

- Make a chart with a big square for every day of the week.
- Choose a category of people for each day.
- Write them onto the chart.
- Pray for them each week on the day you have chosen for them.
- For example:
  Sunday—Pray for family members.
  Monday—Pray for teachers and students and school workers.
  Tuesday—Pray for those who are ill and for doctors, nurses, and other medical staff.
  Wednesday—Pray for those who need to know Jesus, or who are just getting to know Him.
  Thursday—Pray for those who face difficult challenges, such as single parents, those who have experienced abuse, those who feel very alone, or who are struggling with addictions.
  Friday—Pray for your work colleagues and your boss.
  Saturday—Pray for your pastor and his family, and for your church leaders.

- Other categories you might choose could be:
  Those working as missionaries
  Your children's friends
  The church youth leaders and children's program leaders
  Senior citizens
  Your neighborhood
  Your local community

ANOTHER OPTION:
- Instead of a chart, you could create a small book with one page for each day of the week, and illustrate it with the pictures of those you choose to pray for on the different days.

"In the day of trouble he will keep me safe in his dwelling"
(Psalm 27:5).

99

Prayer Cards

It's wonderful to pray for other people, but it's even more encouraging for them when they know that you are praying for them. Send a card that they can keep, which lets them know they are in your thoughts and prayers.

THINGS YOU NEED:
An assortment of purchased blank greeting cards and envelopes
Marker pens
Adhesive
Stickers
Silk flowers
Ribbons and lace
Rubber stamps and inks
Decorative punches and scissors
Computer with graphics program and color printer

- Make special hand-made cards to let people know that you are praying for them.
- Stick a simple, attractive design onto the front of the card and include your message. Maybe you'd like to write out the prayer you prayed for them inside the card.
- Computer greeting card programs can also be used to create cards, or print messages, or even provide you with encouraging words to use in your own cards.
- Stick a miniature teddy bear on the front of a card and send a tiny hug to someone who needs a prayer for comfort or encouragement.
- Stick a Band-Aid onto a card with a prayer for healing.
- Enclose a lace-trimmed handkerchief with your prayer for a woman who has been bereaved.
- Celebrate using bright and happy cards when your prayers for your friends are answered, with prayers of gratitude for what He has done.

"Be kind and compassionate to one another"
(Ephesians 4:32).

73

Email a Prayer

T H I N G S   Y O U   N E E D :
A computer with Internet access
Computer graphics package

- Write out your prayer for a friend and email it to them.
- If you have the skills, create a beautiful PowerPoint presentation of nature photos and encouraging words to send to them.
- Sometimes you can find these presentations on the Internet and forward them to your friends with a prayerful message.
- Search for a Christian greeting company on the Internet, and send an e-card to your friend, adapting the words to include your prayer.

OTHER OPTIONS:
- Send a text message to someone via your cell phone to let your friend know you are praying for them.
- Send a Bible text as a text message to your praying friends each day.

"Do not let any unwholesome talk come out of your mouths, but only what is helpful for building others up according to their needs, that it may benefit those who listen" (Ephesians 4:29).

Newspaper Prayer

THINGS YOU NEED:
A current local newspaper
A marker pen

- As you read through your local paper, draw circles around news items about people and situations that you believe the Holy Spirit is asking you to pray for.
- Look for the good news and thank God for those things.
- Look at the family notices and pray for the families who have new babies, as well as those who have been bereaved.
- Look for information on those who are suffering, and pray for them.
- Ask God to guide you as you pray. Is He asking you to respond to the people and situations in a practical way?

"Like cold water to a weary soul is good news"
(Proverbs 25:25).

75

Button Box Prayer

THINGS YOU NEED:
A box full of all kinds of buttons

- Think of about three or four different people who have helped you in your journey so far as a Christian.
- For each person in turn, try to find a button that somehow represents something about that person, such as the clothes they wore, their special gifts, the way they lived, or the way in which God used them to help you, etc.
- As you hold each button, think of the person that God used to inspire you. Pray for them, if they are still alive, and thank God for their influence in your life.
- Pray that God will somehow use you to influence others in the same way that this person influenced you.
- Perhaps you could write to the person, thanking them for their part in your Christian journey, and letting them know that you have prayed for them.
- Maybe you could even send the button you have chosen with your prayer, and tell them why you chose that button.

ANOTHER OPTION:
- Instead of buttons, use shells on the shore, leaves from trees, stones, etc.

"I have not stopped giving thanks for you, remembering you in my prayers" (Ephesians 1:16).

Recorded Prayer

This is an excellent kind of prayer to make for a special event or to encourage a sick or lonely person.

THINGS YOU NEED:
Portable cassette recorder with a microphone
Blank tape

- Invite different people to pray and record their prayers on the cassette to give to a person, couple, or family.
- At a baby shower, record prayers for a safe birth and for the family's future.
- At a wedding, record a prayer for the couple.
- When someone is moving away from the area, record prayers for their journey, or their new start.
- When a student leaves to go away to college, record prayers for their wisdom and success.
- When someone is sick, record prayers for their comfort, health, and recovery.
- When a pastor is moving to a new church, record prayers of thanks for the ministry of his family in your congregation.
- This kind of prayer can also be encouraging for a shut-in, someone who is isolated, or someone who is facing a difficult challenge.
- Create an attractive cassette cover to slip inside the cassette case, and gift-wrap the cassette before giving it to the person.

OTHER OPTIONS:
- Collect written prayers in an attractive prayer notebook from a Christian bookstore and give the book to the person instead of the cassette.
- Record the prayers on video, and check that you have recorded them in a format that the recipient can receive.

"Therefore encourage one another and build each other up"
(1 Thessalonians 5:11).

77

Prayers for the Road

THINGS YOU NEED:
A drive along the road

- As you drive along the road, pray for the people in the other vehicles.
- Pray for police officers as they face a difficult job. Thank God for the police officers who help to maintain the laws of the community.
- Pray for ambulance workers and firefighters as they rush past you with their sirens screaming and their lights flashing to help people in an emergency. Pray that they'll have wisdom as they work and make the right choices to save people's lives. Pray for the people who need their services, that they will be helped and their lives preserved.
- Thank God for the people driving in cars with Christian symbols on them.
- Thank God for farmers as you pass them in the countryside, growing food for us to eat.
- Pray for the families of the long-distance truck drivers.
- Find ways to pray for the other people whom you pass along the road, or who are stuck with you in traffic jams.

"In all your ways acknowledge him, and he will make your paths straight"
(Proverbs 3:6).

SECTION 9

Prayers for Healing

When the people we know and love are hurt or sick, we want to pray for

them, and we long for them to be healed and happy again. Here are some new

and practical ways to make your prayers more meaningful.

The Leaf Prayer

THINGS YOU NEED:
A bunch of long twigs
A simple vase
Water for the vase
Green card
Hole punch
Garden raffia or twine
Pens
Colored card
Glue
Small basket

- From green card cut lots of leaf shapes about four to five inches long.
- Punch a hole in one end of each leaf.
- Cut the raffia or twine into six- to eight-inch lengths (15-20cm), fold in half and loop-knot the raffia through the hole in each of the leaves.
- Place the leaves in the small basket.
- Write on one of the leaves a simple prayer for someone who needs healing, such as "Please heal Mark's heart after his heart attack."
- Tie the leaf prayer onto one of the twigs.
- Pray daily or weekly for the leaves on the tree.
- When the person has been healed, write the date and the answer on the back of the leaf, and stick a colored card flower onto the front of the leaf close to the punched hole.
- Add more leaves whenever you want to.

OTHER OPTIONS:
- If healing doesn't take place, write other thoughts and prayers on the leaf, such as prayers for comfort and peace for the person who is sick or injured, and their families.
- Encourage others to pray with you for those named on the leaves.

"And the leaves of the tree are for the healing of the nations"
(Revelation 22:2).

79

Plaster Prayer

THINGS YOU NEED:
A permanent marker pen

- Write a simple prayer for healing on the cast of someone who has been injured or had surgery.
- Be sure to ask their permission first, so that you don't cause them any pain or embarrassment.
- Draw a heart or smiley shape on a child's Band-Aid as a symbol of your prayer for their healing.

"I will bind up the injured and strengthen the weak"
(Ezekiel 34:16).

80

Get Well Box

THINGS YOU NEED:
Attractive gift box
Tissue paper
Little items such as listed below
Pen and paper

- Collect little items that symbolize your prayers for the sick person. Wrap them loosely in tissue and put inside an attractive box.
- Write your prayer for the person in a simple way, explaining why you have enclosed the different items.

Some ideas:
- **Small bottle or carton of apple juice** (Song of Solomon 2:5)—May the Holy Spirit refresh you.
- **Tissues or cotton balls**—May the God of all comfort make you feel more comfortable.
- **Small bar of fragrant soap or other fragrant item**—May the fragrance of Jesus fill your room.
- **Packet of raisins** (Song of Solomon 2:5)—May you be strengthened by His love.
- **Something gold colored**—Remember, you are more precious than gold.
- **A small dove**—May His peace be with you.
- **A small candle**—May His light shine upon you in the darkness.

ANOTHER OPTION:
- Do this as a group, and each bring different things, wrapped, and with a prayer label attached. Place them together in a gift box and deliver.

"I was sick and you looked after me"
(Matthew 25:36).

Paper People

THINGS YOU NEED:

Plain paper
"Gingerbread person" cutter
Scissors
Pencil
Large envelopes

- Draw around the gingerbread cutter to make a template.
- Cut out lots of paper-people shapes. You can cut through three to four sheets at once.
- Write the names of sick people on the shapes and then write a prayer for their healing on the back of the shape.
- Write the names of the medical workers you know on some of the paper shapes and write prayers for their work on the back of their shapes.
- Take the envelopes and write on them the names of the different hospitals and clinics in your community. Write "Home" on one of them, for those who are sick at home. Write "Overseas" for the names of countries and missions that you know and pray for.
- Put the different people shapes in their respective envelopes, depending on where they work or are staying at the moment.
- Pray for them regularly, updating prayers as necessary.

"The prayer offered in faith will make the sick person well"
(James 5:15).

82

Bouquet Prayer

THINGS YOU NEED:
Stiff paper in different colors
Marker pens
Adhesive
Scissors

- Create paper bouquet of prayers.
- Cut paper flower shapes out of different colored papers, making the shapes so that the petals can be folded over to cover the center of the flower.
- Write prayers and promises for healing inside the different flowers, fold them up and stick them onto a background, like a vase or as a garland.
- Add leaves and stems with cut paper.
- Let the ill person open up the flowers and read the messages and prayers.

OTHER OPTIONS:
- Do this as a group for someone you know.
- You may like to make templates for the flowers to make it easier. Or look in a children's paper craft book for shape ideas.
- Children could give this to a sick friend. Children like to open up shapes and see what's inside.
- Use this idea to write praises to God instead.

"The wilderness will rejoice and blossom"
(Isaiah 35:1).

International Prayers

This challenging and troubled world needs so many prayers. Here are a

few ideas to help you pray for world issues and those involved in missions

around the globe.

83

Flag Prayers

T H I N G S   Y O U   N E E D :
A book of flags of the world
Paper
Marker pens
Plant stakes
Glue and sticky tape
A vase
Information about different countries
(Flags and information can also be found on the Internet, using a good search engine, and printed out. For information on mission projects, ask different mission organizations what they are doing, or research this on the Internet too.)

- Color in pictures of the flags of different countries in the world. Or print them out on your computer.
- Make the flags large enough so that information about the country's needs and mission projects can be written on the back of the flag.
- Glue or tape the flags onto the plant stakes.
- Place the flags in a vase.
- When you pray for different countries, choose a flag to help you know what to pray for.
- Look for the Christian mission Web sites from that country, to give you ideas for your prayers.
- Add more flags when you find out about other countries that need your prayers.

" 'Go and make disciples of all nations' "
(Matthew 28:19).

84

Missionary Prayer

THINGS YOU NEED:
A real-life missionary family!
Paper
Pens
Envelopes
Postage stamps
Internet access (optional)

- One of the best ways to pray for overseas missions is to know a real-life missionary family.
- Pray that God will guide your family to find a missionary family to pray for.
- Contact a mission organization to give you a list of missionaries you can contact, or, better still, ask around until you find someone who knows a missionary personally.
- Choose a family, and then write to them, telling them that you want to pray for them and you would like to know their prayer needs.
- Pray for the family at least once a week, around their special prayer requests.
- Find other ways to bless and encourage them with gifts and support.

OTHER OPTIONS:
- Encourage other families to find missionary families to pray for and support.
- Ask your whole church to pray for or sponsor a missionary family.
- You may be able to contact your missionary family by email for more up-to-date prayer needs and requests. Email your prayers back to them.

"And not only for that nation, but also for the scattered children of God, to bring them together and make them one" (John 11:52).

85

Map of the World

THINGS YOU NEED:
Globe or map of the world
Removable notes
Pens
Radio/TV/newspapers

- Listen to the news and discover which countries need special prayers during disasters, wars, elections, etc.
- Find the country on your globe or map and write a short prayer on a removable note. Stick the note onto the country and continue to pray for the country during its crisis.
- Don't forget to pray for crises in your own country too.

"The LORD is exalted over all the nations"
(Psalm 113:4).

86

Alphabet World Prayer

THINGS YOU NEED:
An atlas
Books from the library
Information from the Internet
Ring binder with alphabetical index
Paper for binder
Pens

- Choose a different country to pray for each week by taking the next letter in the alphabet and choosing one country that begins with that letter.
- Start with A and pray for Albania. The next week choose B and pray for Bolivia, or another country starting with the letter B.
- Spend some family time each week learning more about the country and its prayer needs.
- Write down your chosen countries, some information about them, and your prayers in a ring binder with an alphabetical index. Add new pages under the different letters as you continue from year to year.
- Look for answers to your prayers and thank God for them.

"'All peoples on earth will be blessed through you'"
(Genesis 12:3).

SECTION II

Take-Away Prayers

Carrying a prayer with us can be a great comfort, and it can remind us to

pray throughout the day.

A Prayer in My Pocket

THINGS YOU NEED:
Buttons of various shapes
Needle and thread

- Often young children feel lonely and afraid when they are away from home and their parents.
- Let your child choose a special button from a selection, and hold it in his or her hand. Talk about how much you love your child, and pray with your child for God's protection and comfort throughout their time away from you. If you can, link the choice of button with the child's special concerns and needs.
- Sew the button inside the child's pocket, where it is secret and hidden, but where the child can feel it whenever they need to be reminded that God is with them. Encourage the child to say a simple, silent sentence prayer to God every time they feel the button.

Button possibilities:
- Heart-shaped—Thank You, God, for loving me.
- Anchor—Please, God, keep me safe.
- Pencil or letter shape—Please, God, help me with my schoolwork and my test.
- Plain round—Thank You, God, for Your love that is all around me and holds me together.
- Smiley face—Thank You, God, for helping me to be happy.

"'Surely I am with you always'"
(Matthew 28:20).

88

A Sticker in My Pencil Case

THINGS YOU NEED:
Child's pencil case
Variety of stickers

- Let the child choose a sticker that reminds them of God's love. Perhaps you could find a suitable sticker in a Christian bookstore.
- Talk about the significance of the sticker, and how it can remind them of your prayers for them at school.
- Have prayer and then stick the sticker inside the pencil case.
- Keep spare stickers in case this sticker falls off or gets lost.

"'Never will I leave you; never will I forsake you'"
(Hebrews 13:5).

A Grace for My Lunch Box

THINGS YOU NEED:
A plain index card
Colored markers and stickers
Access to a laminator

- Help your child to compose a grace prayer for their lunch.
- Write it onto the card, decorate it, and laminate it.
- Stick it inside the lunch box lid using strong adhesive pads, or use adhesive putty if the box lid needs to be put through the dishwasher, so that the grace can easily be removed.

"You prepare a table before me"
(Psalm 23:5).

90

Key-Ring Prayer

T H I N G S   Y O U   N E E D :
A plain key ring
A length of ribbon or light-colored shoelace
Or, a clear plastic key ring into which you can insert a small piece of paper

- Create a key-ring prayer for safe travel.
- Write it onto a length of ribbon or shoelace and thread it through the key ring, or create a key-ring design that will fit into the plastic key ring insert, either written or printed on the computer or stitched.

ANOTHER OPTION:
- If there isn't room for a full prayer, use a symbol such as an angel.

"You discern my going out ... you are familiar with all my ways"
(Psalm 139:3).

SECTION 12

Prayers to Give Away

It's good to share our prayers and use them to encourage and inspire those around us.

Prayer Handkerchief

THINGS YOU NEED:
A plain cotton handkerchief
A piece of paper and a pen, or computer
Sticky tape
Fine-tipped permanent-ink fabric pen

- Compose a short prayer for comfort, especially for a person who is sad. Write it clearly on the paper, or print it on the paper using your computer.
- Make sure the words fit within the edges of the handkerchief.
- Tape the paper with the prayer written on it face up on a washable work surface.
- Tape the handkerchief centrally over the written prayer, making sure it is tightly taped down along all the edges.
- Carefully write the prayer in the handkerchief with a fine pen.
- Iron with a hot iron to set the ink. You don't want tears to make the words run!

OTHER OPTIONS:
- Write the prayer with water-erasable pen and embroider the words using embroidery floss, needle, and embroidery hoop.
- Write a prayer very simply on a good quality paper handkerchief, as a symbol.
- Wrap an attractive handkerchief and write your prayer on the gift label instead of on the handkerchief.

"'He will wipe every tear from their eyes'"
(Revelation 21:4).

Picture Frame Prayer

THINGS YOU NEED:
An attractive picture frame with spaces for two photographs
Photograph of a friend
Paper
Pen
Paints, markers, crayons, etc.
Or computer, scanner, and printer

- Make a prayer picture for a friend.
- Take the photo frame and insert the photo of your friend into one of the spaces.
- Write a special prayer for your friend that will fit into the other space. Use paper and pens, or print the prayer on your computer.
- Decorate the prayer with appropriate decorations.
- Insert the prayer into the other space.
- Wrap and give the photo frame prayer to your friend.

OTHER OPTIONS:
- Scan your friend's photo onto your computer, or use a digital camera and use a photo and print program to create a picture prayer on your computer. This can be framed or laminated as a poster.
- This may make a special gift for a grandparent. Use a picture of your own family and write a prayer from your family for the grandparents.
- Occasionally you can find a novelty picture frame where you can insert a photo and record a short message or prayer that will play when a button is pressed.

"I thank my God every time I remember you ... in all my prayers"
(Philemon 3, 4).

Bookmark Prayer

THINGS YOU NEED:
Card cut into bookmark shapes
Scissors
Rubber stamps
Inks
Stickers and craft materials
Hole punch
Ribbon

- Create a prayer on a bookmark to give to a friend.
- Use all kinds of craft materials to make simple bookmarks.
- Match the theme of the decorations to the theme of the prayer.
- Write a personalized prayer for your friend on the back of the bookmark.
- Punch a hole in the bookmark and knot a length of ribbon through the hole.
- Give the bookmark as a little gift. Or give the bookmark with an encouraging book.

" 'Let the reader understand' "
(Mark 13:14).

Quilt Prayer

THINGS YOU NEED:
You will need to find someone who likes to make quilts
Fabric
Patterns
Fabric pens
Fusible webbing
Batting
Binding
Sewing thread
Embroidery threads

Create a quilt for your child, or for the wall, as a prayer reminder.

- Design a quilt using equal sized squares. Add a half-inch to the finished size of the squares to allow for one-fourth-inch seams.
- Create designs for the squares that remind you of different things to pray about. Many of the traditional quilting designs lend themselves to being prayer reminders.
- For example:
    Angels—prayer for protection.
    Hearts—reminders of God's amazing love.
    Flowers—thanks for God's creation.
    Car—prayer for safe travel.
    House—prayer for the home and family.
    Birds—songs of praise to God.
    Hands and hearts—prayer for God to use our hands to show love to others.
    Flag design—prayer for country.
    Gold Crown—prayer about heaven.
- Appliqué the designs onto the squares, using scrap fabrics and fusible webbing, or use a traditional appliqué method. Borrow quilting books from the library to help you design the appliqués.
- Use fabric pens or embroidery for any words you wish to write on the quilt.

- Sew the finished squares together.
- Make up as a quilt using the instructions from a quilting book.
- Adapt this idea to suit your skills and ideas.

This could be a lovely gift for a new baby.

OTHER OPTIONS:
- Make the quilt up as your prayer for a special friend, or sick person.
- Do this as a group project at a women's prayer group and give the quilt to someone in need of special encouragement.

> *"She makes coverings for her bed"*
> *(Proverbs 31:22).*

Bible Promise Prayer Book

THINGS YOU NEED:
Computer with good graphics program and color printer
Or pens and crayons
White paper
White card
Narrow ribbon and large needle

- Create a booklet of promises that you want to pray for your friend.
- Choose promise verses from the Bible.
- Create pages for the verse book by making large cards on your computer, so that your usual printer paper will print two pages on the front of the paper and two on the back of the paper. Treat each page of the card as a page in the book.
- Match lovely pictures from your computer to the verses that you have chosen for your friend.
- Personalize each page by including your friend's name in the verse.
- Create an attractive cover and print this onto thin card. On the first page explain that the verses are your prayers for your friend.
- Fold the cards in half to form the pages of the booklet and fold the cover around them.
- Sew the book together by making a large stitch through the fold in the book with the ribbon.
- Tie the ends of the ribbon in a bow on the outside of the book.
- Save your designs on the computer and print other books for friends, personalizing them as needed.

" 'I know the plans I have for you,' declares the LORD, 'plans to prosper you and not to harm you, plans to give you hope and a future' "
(Jeremiah 29:11).

96

Huggable Prayer

THINGS YOU NEED:
A plain calico or cotton-covered toy such as a teddy bear
A fine-tipped permanent-ink fabric pen

- Give a prayer that can be hugged!
- Purchase a plain pale-colored, firmly-stuffed soft toy, such as a calico teddy bear.
- Write prayers for the recipient on the bear, either as an individual, or as a group.
- Wrap and give the bear to a mother-to-be, child, someone in need of comfort and encouragement, or even a student leaving home for the first time.

OTHER OPTIONS:
- If you can't find a suitable object for writing on, create your own using simple sewing patterns and plain fabric.
- Find a calico angel to use, and write a prayer for protection on the angel, or on the angel's dress or wings.
- Or purchase a simple calico pillow and write on the cover.

"A time to embrace ..."
(Ecclesiastes 3:5).

97

Sampler Prayer

Sew a prayer sampler as a gift for a wedding, anniversary, new baby, baptism, or other special event.

THINGS YOU NEED:
Purchased embroidery kit with a prayer design
Or, embroidery pattern, suitable fabric, floss, needle, and hoop
Or, a cross-stitch-pattern-creator computer program
Or, squared paper and pencil crayons

- Make up the kit or embroidery following the instructions, or design your own, writing your own prayer to suit the occasion.
- Frame the sampler and give as a gift.
- Keep a photo or copy of the sampler to remind you to pray the same prayer for the person or couple whenever you can.

"A friend loves at all times"
(Proverbs 17:17).

98

Doorknob Prayer

T H I N G S Y O U N E E D :
A blank doorknob sign (the kind that hangs on the doorknob)
Markers, paints, transfers, stencils, etc.

- Create a prayer to hang on someone's door.
- Write a prayer on the blank sign with fine permanent pens.
- Decorate the prayer in any way you like.
- Laminate or seal the sign.

OTHER OPTIONS:
- Laminate a plain cardboard doorknob sign.
- Use nonpermanent wipeable pens to write different prayers on the plain laminated doorknob sign. These can be wiped off and changed regularly.

"Write them on the doorframes of your houses and on your gates"
(Deuteronomy 6:9).

99

Sponsor a Prayer Poster

THINGS YOU NEED:
A skilled graphic designer
Adequate finances
Permission to put up a poster in the area where you wish to place it

- Create a short, meaningful contemporary prayer with high-grade graphics.
- Make a poster to fit a commercial poster space, such as the poster space on a bus, subway train, or phone booth, or sponsor an advertisement in the local paper.
- Pray about the project as a group.
- Raise money to sponsor the project.
- Keep on praying about the prayer project.

ANOTHER OPTION:
- Design T-shirts, mugs, key rings, pens, etc. to promote prayer. Give them as gifts, or sell them to raise money for a ministry project.

" 'Tell them how much the Lord has done for you' "
(Mark 5:19).

100

Prayer Scattering

Bless the people in your workplace with secret prayers.

THINGS YOU NEED:
A large bunch of simple and beautiful flowers
Or, small plants in pots
Or, a box of chocolates or cookies

- Arrive at your workplace early one morning and move from station to station or desk to desk, praying a short, quiet prayer for each worker.
- As you leave their workspace place a flower, cookie, or chocolate on their desk.
- They may never know you prayed, but your prayer could make all the difference to their day, and even their life.
- Your prayers could transform your workplace.

"Let no debt remain outstanding, except the continuing debt to love one another" (Romans 13:8).

Index

Many of the prayer ideas in this book can be adapted to different groups and settings, but some of the ideas have been grouped under different headings to make it easier for you to find a prayer to suit your needs.

You may need to adapt the prayer ideas to suit your group. Know your group well, and be flexible and creative as you prepare special prayer experiences for your group.

Find the prayers by the prayer number below.

Prayer Ideas for Teens

If you enjoyed this book,
you'll enjoy these as well:

It Takes A Church

In *It Takes A Church*, authors Gary L. Hopkins and Joyce W. Hopp, offer practical guidelines and a positive approach to providing spiritual and moral protection for our children by every church member. Here is the information—and the inspiration—to transform your church into the caring community our young people so urgently need.

0-8163-1904-9. Paperback.

US$8.99, Cdn$14.49.

If My People Pray

Randy Maxwell. Using God's counsel in 2 Chronicles 7:14 as a foundation, this book shows how to experience prayer as relationship, power, and the key to revival.

English, 0-8163-1246-X. Paperback. US$10.99, Can$17.99.

Spanish, 1-5755-4031-2. Paperback. US$6.99, Can$11.49.

French, 1-5755-4168-8. Paperback. US$6.99, Can$11.49

Order from your ABC by calling **1-800-765-6955**, or get online and shop our virtual store at **<www.AdventistBookCenter.com>**.

• Read a chapter from your favorite book

• Order online

• Sign up for email notices on new products